W9-CFG-254

CAPTURED HISTORY

FACE OF FREEDOM

HOW THE PHOTOS OF FREDERICK DOUGLASS CELEBRATED RACIAL EQUALITY

by Emma Carlson Berne

Content Adviser: Larry E. Hudson, PhD
Associate Professor of History
University of Rochester

COMPASS POINT BOOKS
a capstone imprint

Compass Point Books are published by Capstone,
1710 Roe Crest Drive, North Mankato, Minnesota 56003
www.mycapstone.com

Editor: Catherine Neitge
Designers: Tracy Davies McCabe and Catherine Neitge
Media Researcher: Svetlana Zhurkin
Library Consultant: Kathleen Baxter
Production Specialist: Laura Manthe

Image Credits
Alamy: Randy Duchaine, 43; Bridgeman Images: The Stapleton Collection/Private
Collection/Frederick Douglass (photogravure), Brady, Mathew (1823-96), 6; Chester
County Historical Society, West Chester, PA, cover, 42, 56 (top); Courtesy of the
National Park Service, Frederick Douglass National Historic Site, Washington, D.C.,
23, 37, 51, 53, 57, 59 (bottom); Getty Images: Bettmann, 11, 25, Corbis, 39,
Corbis/VCG Wilson, 9, Smith Collection/Gado, 21, 40, SuperStock, 5; Granger, NYC,
13, 17, 55; iStockphoto: Andrew_Howe, 52; Library of Congress, 15, 19, 24, 28,
32, 35, 45, 46, 47, 48, 56 (bottom), 58 (bottom), 59 (top); Science Source: Getty
Research Institute, 27; Shutterstock: Everett Historical, 30, 58 (top)

Library of Congress Cataloging-in-Publication Data

Names: Berne, Emma Carlson, author.
Title: Face of freedom : how the photos of Frederick Douglass celebrated racial
equality / by Emma Carlson Berne.
Other titles: How the photos of Frederick Douglass celebrated racial equality
Description: North Mankato, Minnesota : Compass Point Books, a Capstone imprint,
[2018] | Series: Captured history | Includes bibliographical references and index. |
Audience: Grades 4-6. | Audience: Ages 10-12.
Identifiers: LCCN 2017014466| ISBN 9780756556174 (library binding) |
ISBN 9780756556198 (paperback) | ISBN 9780756556211 (ebook pdf)
Subjects: LCSH: Douglass, Frederick, 1818–1895—Juvenile literature. |
Abolitionists—United States—Biography—Juvenile literature. | African American
abolitionists—Biography—Juvenile literature. | Slaves—United States—Biography—
Juvenile literature. | Portrait photography—United States—Social aspects—Juvenile
literature. | United States—Race Relations—Juvenile literature.
Classification: LCC E449.D75 B46 2018 | DDC 973.8092 [B]—dc23
LC record available at https://lccn.loc.gov/2017014466

Printed in the United States of America
010374F17

TABLE OF CONTENTS

Chapter One

PICTURING THE TRUE PERSON

In the spring of 1848, a young black man walked into the photo studio of Edward White in New York City. The young man wanted his picture taken. He was stylishly dressed in a crisp starched shirt and collar, a silk necktie, a vest and a fine black coat. His hair was neatly combed. He was a confident, striking presence, but when he sat for the portrait, he did not meet the camera's gaze. He looked away.

Ten years earlier, Frederick Douglass had been a slave. He had been taught that he was no one, not a real person. He had always refused to believe that. But even now that he was free, showing power was sometimes hard for him. Facing a camera head-on was a powerful thing to do. The past still laid a finger on his shoulder.

It is January 1862. Freezing winds whip the streets of Philadelphia. The United States is in the grip of the Civil War. The famous abolitionist Frederick Douglass sits on a chair in the studio of a friend, the photographer John White Hurn. Three years earlier, Hurn had helped Douglass escape the United States when the authorities threatened to arrest him for aiding in domestic terrorism. Now Douglass sits for Hurn's camera. Again, he wears a fine shirt and cravat. His pose is powerful, commanding. His mouth

Frederick Douglass was photographed in 1862 by his friend John White Hurn. Douglass was in Philadelphia to give a speech on the Civil War.

is set, his eyes are calm and level. His hair is streaked with white now, worn long. He reminds the viewer of a lion, waiting and watching.

Fast-forward to 1877. The Civil War has ended, with the North triumphant. American slavery has ended. And Reconstruction has ended as well. Frederick Douglass is sitting for a portrait by Mathew Brady. The famed photographer documented the Civil War and photographed Andrew Jackson and

Abraham Lincoln. But today he captures the image of the white-haired Frederick Douglass. He wears a full beard now. His face is set in granite lines. He is old and he has done his work—slavery is gone. But some say he's gone soft in his old age. He is financially secure and lives on a grand estate. He commands high prices for his lectures. He has a political

Frederick Douglass was the most photographed American of the 19th century.

appointment—he is the U.S. marshal for the District of Columbia. Some say he has forgotten that black people still struggle. But he might say he has become more practical in his old age.

Frederick Douglass was the most photographed American of the 19th century. From his first photo in 1841 to his deathbed photograph 54 years later, he sat for 160 photographs and daguerreotypes—more even than Abraham Lincoln, who had 126 photographs taken.

Before the mid-19th century, people mostly had their images captured in paintings. Expensive and rare, such pictures were only for the rich. But the daguerreotype changed all that. This early form of photography was inexpensive and easily accessible. Studios cropped up in almost every town and city, and for 25 cents (about $7.50 in today's currency), anyone could have his or her portrait made.

For Douglass, photographs were a democratizing art form. "What was once the exclusive luxury of the rich and great is now within reach of all," he said in a speech. "The humbled servant girl, whose income is but a few shillings per week, may now possess a more perfect likeness of herself than noble ladies and court royalty, with all its precious treasures, could purchase fifty years ago."

Douglass escaped captivity in 1838. Coincidentally, the daguerreotype became much more widely available around the same time. This timing was not lost on Douglass. In his speeches, he linked the birth of his freedom with the birth of photography. He considered photographs powerful truth-tellers. Douglass lived in a world in which black people were almost always depicted in drawings or cartoons as stupid, evil, or silly, or as equivalent to animals, such as monkeys. No one portrayed the black form with dignity or humanity. Certainly no one portrayed black men and women as powerful.

The drawings and cartoons of this time that showed black people are upsetting to the modern eye. In a supposedly humorous lithograph entitled "Grand Football Match-Darktown Against Blackville," monkeylike people with very dark skin are jumbled together in a heap, looking confused. The implication was, of course, that black people were some sort of animal-human hybrid who were not intelligent enough to understand the game. Another picture, a political advertisement, shows two political candidates, for and against allowing black people to vote. The white candidate is shown as sober and neatly groomed. He is wearing a serious expression and a jacket, collar, and tie. The black candidate is depicted with exaggerated facial features, uncombed hair, a mussed, wrinkled shirt, and a silly expression.

It was precisely such insulting images that Douglass sought to refute with his own regal portraits.

DAGUERRE AND EARLY PHOTOGRAPHY

The makers of today's digital images and the photographers of the 20th century owe a great debt to Louis Daguerre, who was a French painter and printmaker. Daguerre spent years with his partner, Nicéphore Niépce, working on a problem no one had yet solved: how to capture an image on a surface, using light and chemicals.

Primitive early cameras had existed for centuries at that point. They were called cameras obscura, and they could project images onto paper. People could trace the images—but how to capture them permanently?

An 1852 daguerreotype of Douglass, taken in Ohio

Niépce figured it out—partially. He dissolved a substance called bitumen in lavender oil and managed to capture an image. But the process was cumbersome, inconsistent, and difficult to reproduce. Enter Louis Daguerre, who performed countless experiments, fiddling and fiddling, until by the 1830s, working alone (Niépce had died), he had managed to develop a consistent, reproducible process for capturing images. Daguerre would coat a thin sheet of copper with silver and sensitize the silver-plated sheet with iodine vapors. After exposing the sheet using a box camera, he would develop the image using mercury fumes. The image was stabilized using salt water.

The process was a big success. But like almost any invention in its early stages, it wasn't without drawbacks. Each daguerreotype was unique, which meant it could not be repeated. There was no way to make copies. And the exposure time was terribly long—the subject had to remain still for five to 30 minutes. Moving would blur the image. For this reason, many early daguerreotypes are pictures of objects instead of people.

In the 1840s others figured out how to reduce exposure times. Variations on the daguerreotype, such as the ambrotype and the tintype, were invented. But Louis Daguerre had done it first, and photographers have owed him a debt ever since.

Photographs could show the true person, Douglass believed. In fact, he thought, they alone were an accurate picture of the man.

Photography could also tell the truth about the horrors of slavery, Douglass believed. Many in the South had a strong belief that slavery was a kind and helpful system, there to help black people who were inherently inferior to white people. Douglass thought photographs forced the viewer to confront the equal humanity of the black person.

In addition, the very accessibility of photography underscored its necessity, according to Douglass. The southern states were sparsely populated and mostly rural—photography was less available there than in the more developed, more urban North. In addition, the southern slave states had more restrictions on free speech and free press, which included photographs. The northern states had no such restrictions.

Frederick Douglass was a writer and an orator. He used his personal story throughout his career to illustrate his abolitionist beliefs. And just as he told stories about his life, he used his own person as an art form. His portraits were a form of expression as much as his words.

"This may be termed an age of pictures," he wrote in the early 1860s. "The sun in his course having turned artist has flooded the world with pictures.

Photographs could show the true person, Douglass believed. In fact, he thought, they alone were an accurate picture of the man.

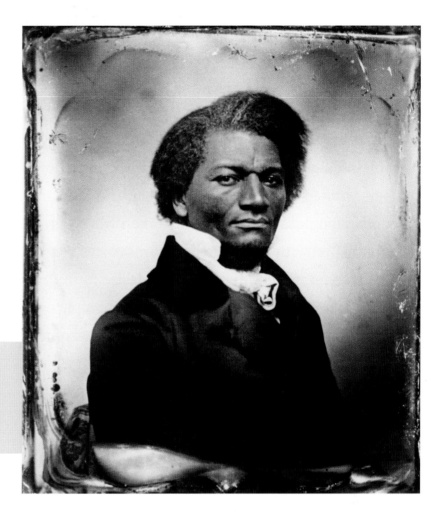

Daguerreotypes, ambrotypes, engravings, and drawings, good, bad, and indifferent, adorn or disfigure, and as frequently the latter as the former, all our dwellings.

"No man thinks of publishing a book without sending his face to the world with it. He may be handsome or homely, manly or otherwise, it makes no difference; the face, the inevitable face, must be there to meet the smiles or frowns of his readers. Once in the book, whether the picture is like him or not, he must forever after strive to look like the picture."

ChapterTwo
SLAVERY TO FREEDOM

Frederick Douglass was a man born into slavery, who by intelligence and massive, churning ambition, pulled—*yanked*—himself out of slavery and into freedom. Douglass was a boy and a man who was never satisfied with his current circumstances. He always wanted more. This perpetual desire for *more* and *better*, not just for himself, but for his people, propelled him from illiteracy and slavery to become one of the great abolitionists of the 19th century.

"From my earliest recollection," he wrote in his autobiography, "I date the entertainment of a deep conviction that slavery would not always be able to hold me within its foul embrace; and in the darkest hours of my career in slavery, this living word of faith and spirit of hope departed not from me, but remained like ministering angels to cheer me through the gloom."

In the eyes of southern society in 1818, only Frederick's body, which could do useful work, had worth. No one cared whether he was smart or stupid, kind or cruel. To his owners, he was a slave and a creature of bondage, just like the cattle in the barns and the horses in the harness. Born a slave in 1818 in a cabin at the edge of a creek in Talbot County, Maryland, Douglass was called Frederick Bailey.

An illustration in Douglass' 1892 autobiography featured the caption: "The last time he saw his mother." His grandmother raised him after he was taken from his mother as a baby. His mother, who walked miles to visit him at night, died when he was young.

He was raised by his grandmother until the age of 8. After that, he worked as a house slave. This was considered a good job—better than working in the fields. Frederick may have been given this job because he was most likely the son of Aaron

Anthony, the plantation owner, and a slave, Harriet Bailey. Douglass later recalled that the Anthony family treated him gently, sometimes patting his head. As a child, he was never beaten.

But Frederick's special status did not shield him from the ugliness all around him. In the autobiography he wrote after his escape, entitled *Narrative of the Life of Frederick Douglass, An American Slave*, he recalls in agonizing detail the sight and sound of a slave being whipped:

"I have often been awakened at the dawn of day by the most heart-rending shrieks of an own aunt of mine, whom [Mr. Plummer, the plantation overseer] used to tie up to a joist, and whip upon her naked back till she was literally covered with blood. No words, no tears, no prayers from his gory victim, seemed to move his iron heart from its bloody purpose. The louder she screamed, the harder he whipped; and where the blood ran fastest, there he whipped longest. He would whip her to make her scream, and whip her to make her hush; and not until overcome by fatigue, would he cease to swing the blood-clotted cowskin. I remember the first time I ever witnessed this horrible exhibition. I was quite a child, but I well remember it. I never shall forget it whilst I remember any thing. It was the first of a long series of such outrages, of which I was doomed to be a witness and a participant. It struck me with awful

An 1863 illustration of an enslaved man being whipped was one of several antislavery cards by Philadelphia lithographer James Fuller Queen.

THE LASH.

force. It was the blood-stained gate, the entrance to the hell of slavery, through which I was about to pass."

Douglass never forgot this sight. He never forgot the other beatings and torture he saw on the farms. He never lost his burning desire to escape slavery.

This lifelong mindset was extraordinary. Other slaves often tried to escape, but Douglass was surrounded by a slave society. Any like-minded people kept their view to themselves. Escape attempts were severely punished by beatings. Slaves were kept illiterate. They were given alcohol to drink on holidays. Frederick liked liquor and the feelings it gave him. But he quickly realized what others did not: the liquor kept slaves drunk and sluggish—they were unable to think of escape or to formulate plots with other slaves.

When Aaron Anthony died, his daughter Lucretia inherited Frederick. She died in 1827, and Frederick's ownership was passed to Thomas Auld, Lucretia's husband. Auld sent Frederick to Baltimore, where he spent seven years working for Hugh Auld, Thomas' brother, and his wife, Sophia.

Frederick had a strong desire to read, and his new mistress, Sophia Auld, taught him his letters— for a time. Hugh soon made her stop. Douglass later recalled that "Mr. Auld found out what was going on, and at once forbade Mrs. Auld to instruct me further, telling her, among other things, that it was unlawful, as well as unsafe, to teach a slave to read." Whites knew that literacy was a threat to the system of slavery because slaves who could read would not depend as much on their owners. Douglass quoted Auld as saying, "A [slave] should know nothing but to

Whites knew that literacy was a threat to the system of slavery because slaves who could read would not depend as much on their owners.

An illustration in Douglass' 1892 autobiography depicts Sophia Auld teaching him to read.

obey his master—to do as he is told to do. Learning would *spoil* the best [slave] in the world."

Frederick did not let that stop him. Out on errands, he would stop white boys on the street and ask them to give him spelling lessons. He and his young teachers would write their words in chalk on doors or barrels, and Frederick would pay them in biscuits.

Soon Frederick was ordered back to the country. Thomas Auld "rented" him to a violent man named

Edward Covey, who was known as a "slave breaker."
While working in the fields for Covey, Douglass,
by then a teenager, was regularly whipped. The
whippings were so violent that flesh as thick as a
finger was stripped from Douglass' back. He referred
to his extremely scarred back years later when he
told northern audiences about the horrors of slavery.

Auld eventually retrieved Douglass from Covey,
but not before more violent fights and beatings that
Douglass would never forget. After an unsuccessful
escape attempt and jail time, Douglass eventually
went back to work for Hugh and Sophia Auld. He
was by then a young man, tall and strong from years
of field work. He labored in the Baltimore shipyards
as a caulker. He enjoyed the greater freedom the job
gave him, but he deeply resented the moment each
week when he had to hand over his pay to Hugh Auld.
It was unfair and degrading, and Douglass never
grew to accept it—just has he had never accepted one
minute of his bondage.

September 3, 1838, marked the most important
day of Frederick Douglass' life. That was the day that
he escaped captivity.

Douglass was familiar with the world of sailors
from his work in the shipyards. From a friend, he
borrowed a sailor's pass, allowing the holder safe
passage on the railroad that ran from Baltimore with
a stop in Philadelphia. After buying a sailor uniform

The 1845 cover of "The Fugitive's Song" sheet music featured Douglass as a runaway slave.

to complete his disguise, and a train ticket, he started his journey northward on September 3.

The trip was extremely risky. At any point, he could have been identified by someone who knew him—and there were many, from his life in Baltimore and his work in the shipyards. He could have been picked up by slave-catchers and returned immediately to bondage, with severe punishment for escaping.

But Douglass was smart and confident. He perfectly acted the role of a sailor who knew just where he was going. He made it to Philadelphia and then to New York, all within 24 hours.

Douglass escaped captivity just as the nation was becoming deeply divided about the question of slavery. To southerners, slavery was essential to their way of life, which was based on agriculture. Without enslaved workers, their economy would collapse. So they promoted the idea that black people were stupid, subhuman, childish, and incapable of caring for themselves. They said black people had to be kept under the care (and bondage) of white people—for their own good.

The growing abolitionist movement in the North vigorously rejected this idea. Slavery was wrong, immoral, sinful, outrageous. Abolitionists thought it could and should be ended, and ended soon. They disagreed about the way to end it, but they all looked toward the same goal. The leading voice for the abolitionists was that of William Lloyd Garrison, a white orator and newspaper publisher in New Bedford, Massachusetts. Garrison was the editor of a highly influential abolitionist newspaper, *The Liberator.* Soon he would come to know an escaped

DOUGLASS' SECOND BIRTH

Frederick Douglass was a vivid, exciting writer who excelled at depicting his own life. In his second autobiography, *My Bondage and My Freedom*, Douglass describes what he considered the turning point of his life and in a sense, his second birth—his arrival in New York as a free man, having escaped captivity. He wrote:

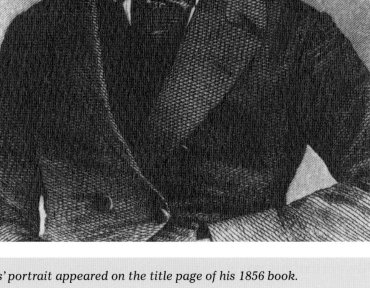

Douglass' portrait appeared on the title page of his 1856 book.

"In less than a week after leaving Baltimore, I was walking amid the hurrying throng, and gazing upon the dazzling wonders of Broadway. The dreams of my childhood and the purposes of my manhood were now fulfilled. A free state around me, and a free earth under my feet! What a moment was this to me! A whole year was pressed into a single day. A new world burst upon my agitated vision. I have often been asked, by kind friends to whom I have told my story, how I felt when first I found myself beyond the limits of slavery; and I must say here, as I have often said to them, there is scarcely anything about which I could not give a more satisfactory answer. It was a moment of joyous excitement, which no words can describe. In a letter to a friend, written soon after reaching New York, I said I felt as one might be supposed to feel, on escaping from a den of hungry lions. But, in a moment like that, sensations are too intense and rapid for words. Anguish and grief, like darkness and rain, may be described, but joy and gladness, like the rainbow of promise, defy alike the pen and pencil. ... I WAS A FREEMAN, and the voice of peace and joy thrilled my heart."

slave named Frederick Douglass, who would become his protégé, and later his rival.

Frederick shed the last name Bailey and adopted the name Douglass, after a character named Douglas in the poem "The Lady of the Lake," by Sir Walter Scott. Douglass added an additional "s" to the spelling. He spent the first three years after his escape working in the boiling hot atmosphere of a brass foundry in New Bedford, Massachusetts. He would nail a newspaper to a post near his workplace so he could read while he operated his bellows. He loved freedom and relished keeping all the money he earned. At last he felt like a man.

Douglass achieved another milestone during this period—he created a family. He had met a free woman named Anna Murray when he was still enslaved, at a party for a debating club for free black people in Baltimore. After his escape, he married Anna and they had five children. During their 44 years of marriage, Anna, who was quiet, hardworking, and illiterate, supported Douglass financially and by caring for their home. He never acknowledged her part in his life, even though she had given him money to buy the train ticket that had brought him out of captivity. For years Douglass lived apart from his family, returning only once in a while, until his youngest children barely recognized him when he came home.

Anna Murray Douglass supported her husband and his work and participated in antislavery activities.

In the summer of 1841, Douglass attended antislavery meetings in Massachusetts. There, for the first time in front of a crowd, he described his experiences as a slave. This was a key moment in Douglass' life. His autobiography describes his appearance before a largely white audience in Nantucket, Massachusetts:

"I felt strongly moved to speak, and was at the same time much urged to do so by Mr. William C. Coffin, a gentleman who had heard me speak in the colored people's meeting at New Bedford. It was a severe cross, and I took it up reluctantly. The truth was, I felt myself a slave, and the idea of speaking to white people weighed me down. I spoke but a few moments, when I felt a degree of freedom, and said what I desired with considerable ease. From that time until now, I have been engaged in pleading the cause of my brethren—with what success, and with what devotion, I leave those acquainted with my labors to decide."

In the audience that day was the well-known abolitionist William Lloyd Garrison. He was impressed with the young man with the commanding presence. He hired Douglass as a speaker for his abolitionist group, the Massachusetts Anti-Slavery Society. And Douglass sat for his first daguerreotype.

Douglass began touring the northern states, speaking to crowds and describing the horrors of slavery. He was immensely popular almost right from the start. It helped that he was a naturally charismatic and talented speaker. He could be humorous and charming. He always wore beautiful clothes. And it is worth noting that most abolitionists, such as Garrison, were white. To have as a speaker a black man, an escaped slave nonetheless, someone who had actually lived through the horrors abolitionists were trying to end, was particularly powerful. Douglass used his body to underscore his message—often referring to his dramatically scarred back.

In 1845, just seven years after his escape,

William Lloyd Garrison

NARRATIVE

OF THE

LIFE

OF

FREDERICK DOUGLASS,

AN

AMERICAN SLAVE.

WRITTEN BY HIMSELF.

BOSTON:
PUBLISHED AT THE ANTI-SLAVERY OFFICE,
No. 25 CORNHILL
1845.

Frederick Douglass

The engraving on the title page of Douglass' autobiography is probably based on a lost daguerreotype.

the Boston Anti-Slavery Office published his autobiography, *Narrative of the Life of Frederick Douglass, an American Slave.* The book was an instant best-seller. For the price of only 50 cents, which was worth about what $16 is today, people could read firsthand about slave life. The book sold 5,000 copies in its first four months. Douglass shot to fame. This time his message reached not just fellow abolitionists, but the American public.

Unfortunately for Douglass, his stories of torture and abuse under bondage also reached down into the

South—to his old masters. Hugh Auld was furious. He vowed to recapture Douglass and send him back to the fields and back to slavery.

Luckily, Douglass had anticipated just this reaction. By the time Auld was calling for his capture, Douglass was safe in Great Britain, where he had fled. He stayed there for nearly two years—and it was while he was in England that he was introduced to the powers of the pictorial press.

For the first time in history, pictures could be regularly published in newspapers, and the *Illustrated London News* was the first successful example of this. Readers could see their news as well as read about it—this had never happened before. Douglass was fascinated. The power of pictures, accompanied by text, could now reach masses of readers. Woodcut prints and drawings were followed by photographs by the end of the century. Douglass himself was featured in drawings twice in the British paper.

When Douglass came home from England in 1847, he was a free man. Supporters had bought his freedom, and he could turn his energy to the idea that had been brewing in his mind for two years. It was time to start his own abolitionist newspaper.

Small newspapers that were published, edited, and owned by an influential abolitionist were extremely important to the antislavery movement. William Lloyd Garrison's paper, *The Liberator,* helped form Douglass' own abolitionist views. Douglass bought a printing press and launched his paper, *The North Star.*

By owning and editing his own newspaper, Douglass hoped to change the minds of naysayers who still believed that a black man didn't have the skills or intelligence to run a newspaper. And he hoped to encourage other black people. "[In] my judgment," Douglass wrote in his second autobiography, *My Bondage and My Freedom,* "a tolerably well conducted press, in the hands of persons of the despised race, by

Douglass (seated at desk) was a featured speaker at the 1850 Fugitive Slave Law convention in New York. The daguerreotype was given to imprisoned abolitionist William Chaplin, who had helped many of the attendees escape to freedom.

calling out the mental energies of the race itself; by
making them acquainted with their own latent powers;
by enkindling among them the hope that for them
there is a future; by developing their moral power; by
combining and reflecting their talents—would prove
a most powerful means of removing prejudice, and of
awakening an interest in them."

The advent of the Civil War caused Douglass to
think, write, and speak even more forcefully about
photography. From 1861 to 1865, he gave four speeches
on photography and the power of pictures. Although
his audiences only wanted to hear about the war,
Douglass insisted on speaking about photography.
He recognized that the Civil War was the first armed
conflict in which photographs could be taken on the

A photograph of soldiers
killed in the Battle of
Gettysburg was titled
A Harvest of Death by its
photographer, Timothy H.
O'Sullivan.

battlefield, giving Americans a visual record of what had happened.

He argued that the wide availability of wartime photographs had directly affected public attitudes toward the war. Photos of Lincoln were published in newspapers and displayed around the country, helping to create the image of Lincoln as a leader who could safely steer the country through unknown waters. The president before Lincoln, James Buchanan, also believed in the power of photographs—he blamed the secession of the southern states on abolitionists who sent photographs through the South, which he thought would inspire slaves to rebel.

In 1855, as rumblings of impending war echoed through the nation, Douglass took a bold step. He and others formed the Radical Abolition Party, a political party that demanded an immediate end to slavery everywhere. At the time, some politicians believed slavery should just not be extended. No, Douglass insisted. It must be rooted out and abolished everywhere it was present. Slavery was a form of war, he thought, and people were obliged to fight to end it.

The party did not shy away from violence. It supported John Brown, a radical abolitionist who seized a federal armory at Harpers Ferry in present-day West Virginia, in 1859 in an attempt to start a slave revolt. Brown was captured, charged with treason, and sentenced to death. Douglass was later implicated as one of Brown's accomplices. He escaped arrest only by fleeing to Canada and Europe.

By June 1860 the charges against Douglass were dropped and the search for accomplices was put aside. Douglass could return to the United States safely. He did, and continued writing, editing, giving speeches, and publishing newspapers throughout the Civil War, which started in 1861. He had accumulated some money and existed in a kind of insulated state, writing from his home in Rochester, New York.

Lincoln signed the Emancipation Proclamation on January 1, 1863. Slaves were freed, he declared, although it would take the end of the war in 1865 to

A newly freed family arrived at a Union army camp in January 1863, shortly after President Lincoln signed the Emancipation Proclamation.

make it a reality for most. Douglass later remembered the moment he heard of the proclamation as the happiest of his life.

The South's defeat in the Civil War and the end of slavery marked another turning point in Douglass' life. Much of what he had worked for had been achieved. But there was still work to be done. He continued traveling almost constantly, giving speeches and lectures. He said his new passion was making it possible for free blacks to vote. From his lectern, he proclaimed that suffrage was the only way to truly free the slaves from their old masters. Nothing since emancipation was as important as the ratification of the 15th Amendment. Winning this right became Douglass' life's work until the amendment, which guaranteed black men the right to vote, was ratified in 1870. Preserving it became the work of the rest of his life.

The issue was not straightforward, however. Suffragists were working hard to gain the right to vote for white women as well. The two movements sometimes converged and sometimes split. Douglass was close friends with suffragist leader Elizabeth Cady Stanton, but he believed that black men should receive the right to vote before white women. Some complained that the influential Douglass supported the women's suffrage movement unenthusiastically. They pointed out how much support women had

From his lectern, he proclaimed that suffrage was the only way to truly free the slaves from their old masters.

THE FIFTEENTH AMENDMENT AND ITS RESULTS.

A portrait of Frederick Douglass (lower left) appeared in an 1870 print commemorating the passage of the 15th Amendment.

given to the antislavery movement. Douglass denied that he had been unenthusiastic. He declared in a letter that "the right of woman to vote is as sacred in my judgment as that of man, and I am quite willing at any time to hold up both hands in favor of this right." However, Douglass went on, "I am now devoting myself to a cause [if] not more sacred, certainly more urgent, because it is one of life and death to the long enslaved people of this country, and this is: negro suffrage."

Douglass spoke out strongly in favor of the Freedman's Bureau—a government agency set up during Reconstruction to help newly freed black people start their lives. Douglass saw the bureau as both a symbolic commitment from the federal government to blacks and as a way for black people to help themselves instead of accepting charity. Douglass felt that black people needed civil rights even more than they needed food, money, and job training. But Douglass may not have known, or may have underestimated, how downtrodden and poor the newly freed slaves were.

Besides trying to help former slaves, Douglass was working hard to join a new establishment of educated black people who were working in government and political parties in Washington, D.C. He craved a political appointment to a government job, and with an eye on that end, he worked to promote the Republican Party in Washington among black people. He got his wish when President Ulysses Grant organized a delegation to consider whether the United States should annex the republic of Santo Domingo—what is now the Dominican Republic. Grant and others thought the land could be used as a sort of black state, to which blacks would be encouraged to move. Grant appointed Douglass to the delegation. But the issue was controversial. Some former abolitionists did not support annexation. The United States should not ship its racial problems to Santo Domingo, they said, but should deal with the problems where they started. Douglass agreed to become secretary of the delegation, whether he agreed with the government position or not. In the end, the government decided not to annex Santo Domingo, but Douglass' actions made his priorities clear—he wanted federal appointments and to some extent, he would do whatever it took to get them.

Douglass stayed active as he grew older. As the most famous black man in the country, he attracted various opportunities. He became the president of the Freedman's Savings and Trust Bank in 1874. Officials of the bank, which was meant for free black people, hoped that Douglass' involvement would allow patrons to trust the bank and keep them from withdrawing their money. Unfortunately, Douglass didn't have wonderful business skills. The bank could not stay afloat financially, and it soon closed. Despite this, Douglass soon received another federal appointment, this one from President Rutherford Hayes. Douglass became U.S. marshal of the District of Columbia, a job that put him in charge of distributing jobs to black civil servants. The U.S. Senate approved his appointment—the first time it had done so for a black man.

Douglass' appointment gave him enough courage in 1877 to travel back to the place where he was once enslaved—Baltimore. There he met with his old master, Thomas Auld, who was dying. Both men were emotional. They met for 20 minutes, talked about the past, and parted in peace.

By now, Douglass was a wealthy man. He never stopped writing and giving speeches, but he became a more settled man, more self-satisfied. Some said he had gotten too rich and a little soft now that he had the kind of federal government job he'd always craved. He had too much money now, his critics complained. He might speak of agitation as a way to achieve an end, but he himself lived in splendor on his 16-acre (6.5-hectare) estate in Washington, D.C. Some felt that Douglass was not sympathetic enough to the plight of poor, uneducated black people who were regularly persecuted.

Douglass had always advocated revolution and resistance—violent when needed. Now he proposed working within the system to change it. In a speech in Lincoln Hall in Washington, D.C., Douglass told the audience, "We should never forget, that, whatever may be the incidental mistakes or misconduct of rulers, government is better than anarchy, and patient reform is better than violent revolution."

This may sound like the voice of one who has forgotten his life mission in favor of money and comfort. But in the very next breath, Douglass showed that he was still the lion he had always been: "But while I would increase this feeling, and give it the emphasis of a voice from heaven, it must not be allowed to interfere with free speech, honest expression, and fair criticism. To give up this would be to give up liberty, to give up progress, and to consign the nation to moral stagnation, putrefaction, and death."

Douglass' wife Anna died in 1882, and he married again—a woman named Helen Pitts who was nearly 20 years younger than he was and white. They had a happy marriage for 11 years. Douglass' fame did not wane. He published his third autobiography. He was appointed by President Benjamin Harrison to be minister to Haiti, which was the first black republic in the world. He received one vote at the Republican national convention in 1888, making him the first

Douglass and his second wife, Helen Pitts, on their 1884 honeymoon to Niagara Falls, New York.

black man to receive a vote for president on a major party's roll call.

Douglass died peacefully of heart failure in February 1895. He appeared to be in excellent health until his death—in fact, his heart attack happened after he returned home from attending a meeting for the National Council of Women.

Throughout his long life, Frederick Douglass never stopped seeking out photographers—friends and strangers—wherever he was. His image was captured over and over, and the photographs never lost meaning for him. But although he knew his photographs had power, he had little idea of their longevity.

ChapterThree
PORTRAITS PROMOTE ABOLITION

The 160 photographs taken of Frederick Douglass share certain similarities when examined by a modern eye. Douglass almost never smiles—this was not uncommon in the days of formal photography, but Douglass made a point of keeping his facial expression stern and dignified. He always wore his best clothes—crisp shirts, neatly tied ties. He wanted to do everything he could to refute the image of the happy, untidy slave.

Fashion at the time dictated the use of many props in photographs—elaborate backdrops, books, pieces of cloth. Douglass preferred plain backgrounds and no props. The few times he did use a prop, it always had special meaning. Once he was photographed with Lincoln's cane. He would sometimes place a book or a newspaper in the shot. He is virtually always alone. Very occasionally he appears with his favorite grandson, Joseph. Twice he appears with his second wife, Helen.

Before the end of slavery, Douglass presents himself in direct, aggressive poses. His fists are sometimes clenched. Or he folds his arms across his chest. He stares directly at the camera. At this time in his life, he advocated violent resistance to slaveholding. After slavery ended, Douglass' poses

Douglass posed for a photo with his grandson Joseph, who became a famed concert violinist.

soften. He sometimes gazes to the side of the lens. He is growing older. He has achieved his goal.

Douglass looks directly at the camera or to the side. Occasionally he is shot in profile. Always he models an amazing variety of styles—long hair, usually; a goatee; a chin beard; a mustache; muttonchop side whiskers; clean-shaven; a full beard. He even has a short ponytail at one point. At the time, elaborate, sometimes eccentric hairstyles were popular among intellectuals. It was as if the wearer's body could not contain his thoughts—they were sprouting out of him, even through his hair.

The viewer watches Douglass' face grow lined over the years, his hair grow white. He never loses his dignity, not even in the last photograph taken of him—that of his body on his deathbed.

One of the only known photographs of Douglass smiling was taken in 1894 in New Bedford, Massachusetts.

Douglass had Louis Daguerre to thank for these photographs. The French photographer invented the first method of reliably creating a good photograph. Images were printed on thin sheets of metal, and the chemicals and equipment needed were easy to get and not very expensive. By the late 1850s, almost every city and many small towns in the United States had a photographic studio.

Portraits were what people wanted—about 90 percent of all the images taken during the latter half of the 19th century were portraits. People requested photos of their children, their extended families, and their sons going off to fight in the Civil War.

The photographers were spread widely across the country—at nearly every city or town where Douglass spoke, he would stop into a local studio for a photograph.

In a speech, "Pictures and Progress," Douglass described some of the moveable studios he saw on his travels: "The smallest town now has its Daguerrian Gallery; and even at the cross roads—where stood but a solitary blacksmith shop and what was once a country tavern but now in the last stages of [dilapidation]—you will find the inevitable Daguerrian Gallery. Shaped like a baggage car, with a hot house window at the top—adorned with red curtains resting on … springs and wooden wheels painted yellow. The farmer boy gets an iron shoe for his horse, and metallic picture for himself at the same time, and at the same price. ... The facilities for travel [have] sent the world abroad—and the ease and cheapness with which we get our pictures has brought us all within range of the daguerrian apparatus."

One such portrait photographer, Edward White, made a daguerreotype of Douglass at White's New York City studio in 1848. White also had a small business that made daguerreotype equipment. Little is known about White aside from his business ventures. He ran studios in New York and New Orleans, Louisiana, and at one point he organized an exhibition of 1,000 miniature daguerreotypes of famous men.

When White took Douglass' photo, the abolitionist was in New York to attend a meeting of the American Anti-Slavery Society, and also to give a speech at Convention Hall, which was near White's studio.

The daguerreotype shows a 30-year-old Douglass. His face is smooth, and there are no signs of the harsh lines of later years. His hair is trimmed and neatly side-parted, in the style of the day. His features are as striking and handsome as they always would be— hawk-bridged nose, finely cut lips, straight eyebrows, high cheekbones, and narrow eyes. Douglass looks down and away from the camera—he has not yet refined the aggressive stance of later years. He wears fine clothes in the fashion of the day—an upstanding collar tied with a silk necktie, a buttoned white shirt,

Frederick Douglass in 1848. The daguerreotype was taken by Edward White.

silk vest, and a nattily tailored black coat. What is most likely a watch chain is visible under his coat and on top of his vest.

Everything about Douglass suggests that this man is a gentleman—aside from the gaze, nothing remains of the slave Frederick Bailey. He later gave a copy of the daguerreotype to the women's suffrage activist Susan B. Anthony.

Statues in Susan B. Anthony Square in Rochester, New York, depict the suffragist and her friend Frederick Douglass having tea.

Douglass owed a significant debt to another photographer, John White Hurn. In October 1859, the radical abolitionist John Brown had led a raid on a federal store of weapons in Harpers Ferry, in present-day West Virginia. Brown was captured, and Frederick Douglass and others were implicated in aiding him. The sheriff in Franklin County ordered his arrest.

Douglass had just arrived in Philadelphia to give a speech. The sheriff sent a telegraph message to the sheriff of Philadelphia. Luckily for Douglass, the telegraph operator who received the message was the Douglass sympathizer John White Hurn. He delayed delivery of the telegram for three hours. Meanwhile, he sent a message to a local Underground Railroad operator, who found Douglass and warned him of his imminent arrest. Douglass received the message in time and left for Rochester, New York, immediately by train. He then left the country, bound for Canada and England.

But Douglass did not forget Hurn, and when he returned to the United States, he honored his friend by sitting for him several times—in 1862, 1866, and 1873. Hurn took nine portraits of Douglass, more than any other photographer.

Hurn's 1862 photograph of Douglass was published in the form of a carte-de-visite. The small photographs were invented in 1854. A print was

In 1862 John White Hurn photographed Douglass at his Philadelphia studio after Douglass' safe return to the United States.

mounted on a sheet of cardstock, to be placed in photo albums or given as gifts. Because they were printed on paper, as opposed to metal like daguerreotypes, they were inexpensive and easy to mail.

The carte-de-visite that Hurn made of Douglass shows an older and more weathered man than the smooth-faced gentleman of 1848. Douglass is now 44—solidly middle-aged. His hair is long, brushed back, and streaked with white and gray. The lines of his face are set, and his eyes are level, confident, and worldwise. He looks like the intellectual he was—not just a gentleman, but a thinking man whose ideas mattered to other people.

Mathew Brady was perhaps the most famous photographer to capture Douglass. Considered the first photojournalist, Brady became well-known after taking photographs on Civil War battlefields.

Douglass sat for Brady in 1877 when he was 59 years old. His hair and full beard are completely white. He wears them long, as was his style. In this picture,

Brady's stereographic image of Douglass was made to be seen through a special viewer. The image would seem to be in three dimensions. The 3-D photos were very popular at the time.

CIVIL WAR PHOTOGRAPHER

Mathew Brady photographed a wounded soldier in a deserted Army camp in 1865.

Born to Irish immigrants in about 1823, Mathew Brady learned how to make daguerreotypes from Samuel Morse, who invented the telegraph. Brady was a prominent photographer and took the portraits of many famous people, including former first lady Dolley Madison, former President Andrew Jackson, and future presidents Millard Fillmore and Abraham Lincoln.

When the Civil War began, Brady took advantage of new, more portable photography equipment. He organized a group of photographers who traveled directly to the battlefields. There he and his employees photographed the camps, the marches, and dead soldiers, lying where they had fallen.

No one had ever seen photographs like them before. For the first time, the visual horrors of war were brought directly to people's homes. "Mr. Brady has done something to bring home to us the terrible reality and earnestness of war," *The New York Times* said in 1862. "If he has not brought bodies and laid them in our dooryards and along the streets, he has done something very like it."

After the war, Brady continued taking photographs, but he had fallen into serious debt. Two years before he took Frederick Douglass' portrait, he had sold several thousand of his negatives to the U.S. government for $25,000. The Library of Congress has more than 7,000 Civil War images from Brady and other photographers available online.

Douglass is shot in three-quarter view. His face is softer, the lines less harsh. He wears neat, fashionable clothes, including a carefully knotted silk bowtie and a silk vest decorated with polka dots.

The same year this photograph was taken, Douglass bought a beautiful estate in Anacostia, a neighborhood in Washington, D.C. The brick house overlooked 16 acres (6.5 hectares) of lawns and gardens. Douglass had become a wealthy man. Even after three decades in the public spotlight, he could still command as much as $300 per lecture—about $7,000 in today's money. Some people thought he had grown soft in his comfortable later years. The Civil

Douglass'
photos were
not for his
personal use,
and he did not
mean them
to be.

War was long over, slavery had been abolished, and Reconstruction—the period of rebuilding the country after the Civil War—was ending. Douglass had settled into an elder statesman role. He no longer pushed for radical, violent revolution. Instead he told his listeners that governmental reform was the way forward. But to some, it seemed that Douglass had forgotten the thousands of black people who lived in poverty and faced discrimination.

Douglass' photos were not for his personal use, and he did not mean them to be. They were public, and they were meant to be part of his public persona. Douglass used his photographs as a sort of visual personal narrative, which told his story in much the same way that his three autobiographies did.

The photographs were immensely popular. From pictures of the interiors of people's homes we know that even many Americans who did not personally know Douglass had a photograph of him in their home.

Douglass sold his photographs and gave the money to abolitionist organizations. He published them on posters and in newspapers to promote his talks. He even used his photograph to gain subscriptions to one of his newspapers—new subscribers got a free photo.

For Douglass, his portraits and his words were linked. The photographs helped convey his words and molded his public image. Both were part of the abolitionist narrative he spread.

ChapterFour
LASTING SYMBOL OF RESISTANCE

Frederick Douglass wasn't alive in the last photograph taken of him. He died February 20, 1895, at the age of 77. Photographs and sculptures of the dead, in the form of molded masks, were very popular at the time. Douglass' deathbed photo was most likely taken a day after he died. It is a peaceful photograph. Douglass lies on a bed, his head propped on a pillow. His hands are crossed on his abdomen, and his eyes are closed. His long white hair is neatly spread behind him. He wears a white nightshirt—a startling contrast to the sober black clothes he wore during his life.

He is still magisterial, and this photograph, like all the others, was widely distributed. Newspapers across the country published Douglass' obituary, and some included his deathbed picture. "Death of Fred Douglass," said the headline over a front-page *New York Times* story on February 21, 1895. It continued: "Frederick Douglass dropped dead in the hallway of his residence on Anacostia Heights this evening at 7 o'clock. He had been in the highest spirits, and apparently in the best of health, despite his ... years, when death overtook him."

The face of the famous abolitionist quickly became a symbol for the black struggle. Soon after his death, an artist featured Douglass' face on the side of a glazed

50

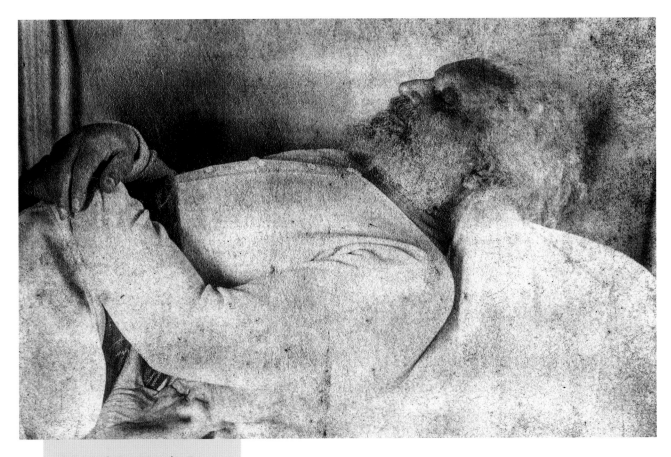

ceramic pitcher. His image was placed inside the cornerstone of a school, along with other symbolic items. Small pictures and engravings of Douglass were printed by the thousands and used to promote abolitionist causes.

The image of Douglass was not forgotten after the end of the 19th century. A mural of Douglass surrounded by other black historical leaders and images of slavery graces a wall in Belfast, Northern Ireland. Douglass' face appears along with those of Malcolm X, Martin Luther King Jr., and civil rights activist Ella Baker on the wall of a stretch of row houses in Philadelphia. A grand mural of Douglass was painted on the wall of a large building in Washington, D.C.

Life magazine placed one of his daguerreotypes on its cover in 1968 under the headline "The Search for a Black Past." He gazes out magisterially from a 32-cent U.S. postage stamp in 1995, holding his finger aloft as if about to impart some great wisdom to us. In 1945, the International Fur and Leather Workers Union used his face on a flyer, along with the Douglass quote "The lesson of the ages is that a wrong done to one man is a wrong done to all men."

His image has not lost meaning for artists, who manipulate his portraits, repaint them, make collages out of them. He stands against his own words on a wall in Rochester, New York. "Without struggle, there can be no progress," hand-painted words declare beside a reproduction of one of John White Hurn's daguerreotypes. A person in the 21st century can easily buy a Frederick Douglass T-shirt with his image emblazoned below the word "Respect."

There is no doubt that Douglass has carved out his place in the American consciousness as one of the great leaders for black rights. But with the cultivation of his image, he has done more than that. He has given the public a visual hook on which to hang their images of black humanity. He symbolizes struggle and change, militant resistance as well as measured reform. And perhaps this is a product of the sheer

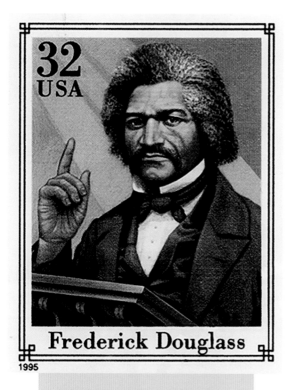

A U.S. stamp was based on an 1864 photo. In the photo, Douglass' finger is pointing down, not up.

ANNA MURRAY & HELEN PITTS

Frederick Douglass—the abolitionist, lecturer, author, and public speaker—never had much in common with Anna Murray, his wife of 44 years. He often did not live with her and their children. His life was consumed with his work, which was the way he preferred it.

Anna was five years older than Douglass and a free black woman when they met in Baltimore. She never learned to read or write, but she could play the violin beautifully and she taught Frederick how to play. They met at a meeting of the East Baltimore Mental Improvement Society, a club for free black men and women. They were married on September 15, 1838.

Anna looked up to her educated, naturally elegant husband. He did not treat her the same. Not cruel, by any means, but he always regarded her with a certain indifference. He did call her his "helpmeet," but for the most part, Anna was simply useful to him. She ran his household, cared for their children, and came when he summoned her. They had five children—Rosetta (1839–1906), Lewis Henry (1840–1908), Frederick (1842–1892), Charles Remond (1844–1920), and Annie (1849–1859).

Douglass' relationship with his second wife, Helen Pitts, could not have been more different. Helen was his former secretary and was 20 years younger than him— and she was white. Interracial marriage was rare in those days, and often illegal. Both blacks and whites were upset

Douglass posed in 1884 with his wife, Helen (seated), and her sister Eva.

by their union. But unlike Frederick and Anna, Frederick and Helen had a true partnership and many shared interests. Helen had a college education and loved to read and travel. She and Douglass visited England, France, Italy, Greece, and Egypt together. Douglass sat for photographs with Helen as well. In one, he sits magnificently at a small table, facing the camera with a slight smile, his hair long and white. Helen sits opposite him, her elbow on the arm of her chair, gazing at him adoringly. Helen's sister stands behind the table. Not a single photo exists of Frederick and Anna.

number of his speeches, writings, and images—there are so many that nearly every group that works for justice can find words spoken or written by him or pictures of him that support their cause.

The scholar Henry Louis Gates Jr. writes that "Douglass was intent on the use of this visual image to erase the astonishingly large storehouse of racist stereotypes that had been accumulated in the American archive of anti-black imagery, the bank of simian and other animal-like caricatures meant to undermine the Negro's claim of common humanity, and therefore the rights to freedom and citizenship and economic opportunity."

Douglass was acutely aware of the extraordinary power of one person. He chose to use his power, intelligence, and charisma to fight for justice, like the great civil rights leaders who followed him. He could have chosen a different life. He could have chosen to remain a slave and not risk being killed when trying to escape. He could have chosen not to educate himself. He could have chosen to work the bellows at the New Bedford foundry for the rest of his days.

But he did not choose any of those paths. He chose freedom, resistance, and education, and he was determined and resolute in advocating those for others. And Douglass made another far-reaching decision— he chose to use himself as a symbol. By having his portrait taken and distributed, Douglass was making

He chose to use his power, intelligence, and charisma to fight for justice, like the great civil rights leaders who followed him.

Frederick Douglass, the great abolitionist, fought for justice his entire life.

the point that he was a citizen and a human as much as any other person. He was giving himself power and insisting that others recognize that. He was relentless in this. And his plan worked—most likely beyond his wildest dreams. Frederick Douglass was a symbol in his own day, but his influence extended far beyond his life—indeed, beyond his own century. He has not been forgotten in the 21st century. His words and his images remain powerful—likely for decades, even centuries to come.

Timeline

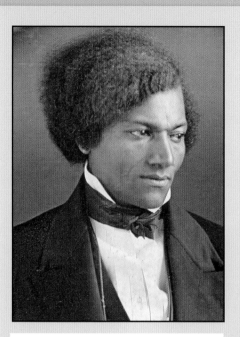

1819–1825

After being separated from his mother, Douglass lives with his grandmother, Betsey Bailey; in 1827 he is sent to live in Baltimore with Hugh and Sophia Auld, where Sophia teaches him the alphabet

1818

Frederick Douglass is born as Frederick Bailey in February in Talbot County, Maryland; his mother, Harriet Bailey, was enslaved; his father, a white man, is believed to be slave-owner Aaron Anthony

1841

At the urging of abolitionist William Lloyd Garrison, Douglass speaks to an audience at an antislavery meeting in Nantucket, Massachusetts; he begins work for the Massachusetts Anti-Slavery Society

1834

Douglass is sent to learn field work from "slave breaker" Edward Covey; he tries to escape in 1836, but his plot is discovered and he is jailed

1836–1838

Douglass works at the Baltimore shipyards

1838

Douglass escapes to freedom using the Underground Railroad and heads to New York City; he marries Anna Murray on September 15 and settles in New Bedford, Massachusetts

1845

Douglass' first autobiography, *Narrative of the Life of Frederick Douglass, An American Slave,* is published; he leaves for Ireland and England to avoid arrest as a fugitive slave; money is raised to buy his freedom

1847

Douglass returns from England a free man and moves to Rochester, New York; he founds the abolitionist newspaper, *The North Star*; the next year he begins sheltering escaped slaves in his house as part of the Underground Railroad

Timeline

1855

Douglass' second autobiography, *My Bondage and My Freedom*, is published; his third autobiography, *Life and Times of Frederick Douglass*, is published in 1881

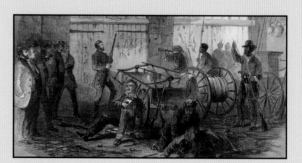

1859

John Brown raids the federal arsenal at Harpers Ferry, while trying to start a slave revolt; Brown is captured and executed; Douglass is implicated as an accessory; he escapes to Canada and England to avoid arrest

1865

The Civil War ends; Lincoln is assassinated; the 13th Amendment to the Constitution, which outlawed slavery, is adopted; Douglass was later appointed to various government positions

1872

Virginia Woodhull's Equal Rights Party nominates Douglass for vice president, but he declines; he moves with his family to Washington, D.C.

1882

Anna Murray Douglass dies August 4, at the age of 69

1860

Abraham Lincoln is elected president; Douglass returns to the U.S.; South Carolina secedes from the Union; the Civil War begins the next year; Douglass calls for African-Americans to be included in the Union Army

1863

President Lincoln signs the Emancipation Proclamation, declaring slaves in the Confederate states that were still in rebellion to be free; Douglass serves as adviser to Lincoln

1884

Douglass marries Helen Pitts on January 24; they tour Europe and Northern Africa in 1886 and 1887

1895

Douglass suffers a heart attack and dies on February 20 at his home in Washington, D.C.; he was 77

Glossary

abolitionist—person who supported the banning of slavery

ambrotype—early type of photograph, made by placing a glass negative against a dark background

caulker—person who seals the seams of boats

charisma—special magnetic charm or appeal

daguerreotype—early photographic process in which an image is produced on a silver-coated copper plate

illiterate—unable to read or write

inevitable—certain to happen; unavoidable

lithograph—picture printed using a stone or metal block on which an image has been drawn with a thick substance that attracts ink

orator—skilled public speaker

persona—the aspect of someone's character that is presented to others

pictorial—newspaper or magazine that has pictures as its main feature

protégé—person who is guided and supported by an older and more experienced or influential person

Reconstruction—period after the Civil War, from 1865 to 1877, when the federal government governed states in the former Confederacy and granted rights to and protected African-Americans

secession—the withdrawal of 11 southern states from the Union in 1860 and 1861, leading to the Civil War

simian—relating to monkeys or apes

suffrage—the right to vote

tintype—early type of photograph made on a piece of metal

Additional Resources

Further Reading

Condon, Robin L. *All About Frederick Douglass*. Indianapolis: Blue River Press, 2016.

Freedman, Russell. *Abraham Lincoln and Frederick Douglass: The Story Behind an American Friendship*. Boston: Houghton Mifflin Harcourt, 2012.

Maloof, Torrey. *True Life: Frederick Douglass*. Huntington Beach, Calif.: Teacher Created Materials, 2017.

Prince, April Jones. *Who Was Frederick Douglass?* New York: Grosset & Dunlap, 2014.

Internet Sites

Use FactHound to find Internet sites related to this book.
Visit *www.facthound.com*
Just type in 9780756556174 and go.

Critical Thinking Questions

Frederick Douglass argued that photographs could show the true humanity of a person better than drawings or paintings. Do you agree with this view? Why or why not?

This book often uses Douglass' own words in quotations. Why do you think the author included so many quotes?

In Chapter 1, the author describes several offensive racial cartoons and drawings. How did reading those descriptions make you feel? Now read the descriptions of Douglass' photographs in Chapter 3. How do those descriptions make you feel? What do you think Frederick Douglass himself would have said about the contrast between those feelings? Support your answers with evidence from the text.

Source Notes

Page 7, line 20: Frederick Douglass. "Pictures And Progress: An Address Delivered In Boston, Massachusetts, on 3 December 1861." Frederick Douglass Papers Digital Edition. 30 Jan. 2017. http://frederickdouglass. infoset.io/islandora/object/ islandora%3A2179#page/1/ mode/1up

Page 10, line 26: John Stauffer, Zoe Trodd, and Celeste-Marie Bernier. *Picturing Frederick Douglass: An Illustrated Biography of the Nineteenth Century's Most Photographed American.* New York: Liveright Publishing Corporation, 2015, p. 142.

Page 11, caption: Frederick Douglass. Heilbrunn Timeline of Art History. Metropolitan Museum of Art. 1 May 2017. http://www.metmuseum.org/ toah/works-of-art/2001.756/

Page 12, line 10: Frederick Douglass. *Narrative of the Life of Frederick Douglass, An American Slave.* Boston: The Anti-Slavery Office, 1845, p. 31. http://docsouth.unc.edu/neh/ douglass/douglass.html

Page 13, caption: Frederick Douglass. *The Life and Times of Frederick Douglass.* Boston: De Wolfe, Fiske & Co., 1892, p. 37. http://docsouth.unc.edu/neh/ dougl92/dougl92.html

Page 14, line 11: *Narrative of the Life of Frederick Douglass, An American Slave*, p. 6.

Page 16, line 21: Ibid, p. 33.

Page 16, line 28: Ibid.

Page 21, col. 1, line 13: Frederick Douglass. *My Bondage and My Freedom.* New York and Auburn: Miller, Orton & Mulligan, 1855, p. 336. http://docsouth.unc.edu/ neh/douglass55/douglass55.html

Page 23, line 8: Ibid., p. 117.

Page 27, line 7: Ibid., p. 389.

Page 32, line 3: William S. McFeely. *Frederick Douglass.* New York: Norton & Co., 1991, p. 268.

Page 36, line 5: Frederick Douglass. "The Civil Rights Case." 22 Oct. 1883. 11 Jan. 2016. http://teachingamericanhistory. org/library/document/the-civil- rights-case/

Page 36, line 13: Ibid.

Page 41, line 20: "Pictures And Progress: An Address Delivered In Boston, Massachusetts, on 3 December 1861."

Page 47, col. 2, line 3: "Brady's Photographs: Pictures of the Dead at Antietam." *The New York Times.* 20 Oct. 1862. 11 Jan. 2016. http://www. nytimes.com/1862/10/20/news/ brady-s-photographs-pictures- of-the-dead-at-antietam. html?pagewanted=all

Page 50, line 15: "Death of Fred Douglass." *The New York Times.* 21 Feb. 1895, p. 1. http://www. nytimes.com/learning/general/ onthisday/bday/0207.html

Page 51, caption: *Picturing Frederick Douglass: An Illustrated Biography of the Nineteenth Century's Most Photographed American*, p. 226.

Page 52, line 4: "The Search for a Black Past." *Life.* 22 Nov. 1968. 30 Jan. 2017. https://books.google. com/books?id=-VMEAAAAMBA J&printsec=frontcover&source=g bs_ge_summary_r&cad=0#v=one page&q&f=false

Page 52, line 10: *Picturing Frederick Douglass: An Illustrated Biography of the Nineteenth Century's Most Photographed American*, p. 106.

Page 54, line 6: Ibid., p. 209.

Select Bibliography

"A Brief History of the Carte de Visite." The American Museum of Photography. 30 Jan. 2017. http://www.photographymuseum.com/histsw.htm

"Brady's Photographs: Pictures of the Dead at Antietam." *The New York Times*. 20 Oct. 1862. 11 Jan. 2016. http://www.nytimes.com/1862/10/20/news/brady-s-photographs-pictures-of-the-dead-at-antietam.html?pagewanted=all

Daniel, Malcolm. "Daguerre (1787–1851) and the Invention of Photography." Heilbrunn Timeline of Art History. The Metropolitan Museum of Art. October 2004. 30 Jan. 2017. http://www.metmuseum.org/toah/hd/dagu/hd_dagu.htm

Douglass, Frederick. "The Civil Rights Case." 22 Oct. 1883. 11 Jan. 2016. http://teachingamericanhistory.org/library/document/the-civil-rights-case/

Douglass, Frederick. *My Bondage and My Freedom*. New York and Auburn: Miller, Orton & Mulligan, 1855. http://docsouth.unc.edu/neh/douglass55/douglass55.html

Douglass, Frederick. *Narrative of the Life of Frederick Douglass, An American Slave*. Boston: The Anti-Slavery Office, 1845. http://docsouth.unc.edu/neh/douglass/douglass.html

Douglass, Frederick. "Pictures And Progress: An Address Delivered In Boston, Massachusetts, on 3 December 1861." Frederick Douglass Papers Digital Edition. 30 Jan. 2017. http://frederickdouglass.infoset.io/islandora/object/islandora%3A2179#page/1/mode/1up

Douglass, Frederick. "The Trials and Triumphs of Self-Made Men: An Address Delivered in Halifax, England, on 4 January 1860." 30 Jan. 2017. http://frederickdouglass.infoset.io/islandora/object/islandora%3A1948#page/2/mode/1up

Greenspun, Philip. "History of Photography Timeline." Photo.net. January 2007. 30 Jan. 2017. http://bclearningnetwork.com/LOR/media/Photo12/U1-History/History_of_Photography_Timeline.pdf

Guterl, Matthew Pratt. "Frederick Douglass's Faith in Photography." *The New Republic*. 2 Nov. 2015. 30 Jan. 2017. https://newrepublic.com/article/123191/frederick-douglasss-faith-in-photography

"John Brown." Africans in America: Judgment Day. PBS Resource Bank. 30 Jan. 2017. http://www.pbs.org/wgbh/aia/part4/4p1550.html

"Mathew Brady: Photographer." Civil War Trust. 30 Jan. 2017. http://www.civilwar.org/education/history/biographies/mathew-brady.html

Stauffer, John. *Giants: The Parallel Lives of Frederick Douglass & Abraham Lincoln*. New York: Twelve, 2008.

Stauffer, John, Zoe Trodd, and Celeste-Marie Bernier. *Picturing Frederick Douglass: An Illustrated Biography of the Nineteenth Century's Most Photographed American*. New York: Liveright Publishing Corporation, 2015.

Thompson, Julius E., James L. Conyers Jr., and Nancy J. Dawson, eds. *Frederick Douglass Encyclopedia*. Santa Barbara, Calif.: Greenwood Press, 2010.

Wilson, Lillian. "19th Century Photographic Processes and Formats." Captured by the Camera: 19th century photographic portraits of Concord people. The Concord Free Public Library. 30 Jan. 2017. http://www.concordlibrary.org/scollect/portrait_exhibit/notes.html

Index

About the Author

Emma Carlson Berne has written many historical and biographical books for children and young adults. She lives in Cincinnati with her husband and three sons.